To

ben --

gratitude always

Doug

CONNECTING WITH RESISTANT TEENAGERS

10 PROVEN STEPS

by

Anna Russo

EDUCATION DEGREE from ITALY
LIFE COACH, NLP TRAINER

Bloomington, IN  Milton Keynes, UK

authorHOUSE®

AuthorHouse™
1663 Liberty Drive, Suite 200
Bloomington, IN 47403
www.authorhouse.com
Phone: 1-800-839-8640

AuthorHouse™ UK Ltd.
500 Avebury Boulevard
Central Milton Keynes, MK9 2BE
www.authorhouse.co.uk
Phone: 08001974150

© 2006 Anna Russo. All rights reserved.

No part of this book may be reproduced, stored in a retrieval system, or transmitted by any means without the written permission of the author.

First published by AuthorHouse 8/23/2006

ISBN: 1-4259-5072-8 (sc)

Printed in the United States of America
Bloomington, Indiana

This book is printed on acid-free paper.

Table of Contents

TEN TECHNIQUES – A CHECKLIST

1. Being a good model does not guarantee children will listen. Parents need to learn to ask the right questions and focus on the right issues.

2. Learn how to ask engaging questions. Good intentions simply are not enough to raise happy and well-adjusted children. Good communication is essential to a peaceful and happy home. Decide on the outcome and the message you want to deliver.

3. Peer pressure is an extremely strong force in shaping children's behavior. Creativity and objectivity on the parents' part can help route the peer pressure in a positive direction.

4. We are motivated by what we value. Parents need to accept that children have their own pressures. Using techniques to link a feeling of accomplishment to doing a good job is a necessary strategy to learn and apply in order to motivate children.

5. High expectations for children based on what we think they should do can be easily deflated. Changing reaction to action is the way to inspire our children.

6. Setting appropriate boundaries is a must if you want to raise well-grounded children. Respectful communication and realistic expectations can rid your home of chaos and frustration.

7. The proper strategies help children change their behavior and boost their self-worth. Help them think by asking questions, and give them a chance to review their thought process.

8. Children are all unique individuals, and grow up at different stages. Parents need to communicate with each child according to that child's focus and style.

9. When you connect with your children at their level, you show them that you care. You will be able to maintain rapport, and they will be more open to your suggestions.

10. If you find yourself living in a combined family, the goal is to develop the same respect, objectivity and patience with your spouse's children as with your own.

Introduction

I recommend that you read this book with an **open mind** and with the purpose of assisting yourself to be the best parent you can be. Give yourself the flexibility to explore your own family dynamic. Allow yourself the permission to be comfortable with the process of looking at some areas of your communication in a new way.

As I present situations, I will give you suggestions and strategies to add to your current skills that will guarantee better results. Children do not come with an owner's manual; they are unique like fingerprints. Imagine having powerful new tools and strategies to make the changes that you have been wishing to make for a long time! This book is designed to be brief and concise for immediate results in a time-pressured world. By now you have realized that **wishing** is not going to make anything happen. To create the results you really want, you need different strategies, new perspectives and precise communication skills.

Throughout this book you will be presented with a different way of communication than that to which you are accustomed. Studies have proven that words do influence the brain. Even though tone of voice has a stronger effect, words create images in your mind, like, "Can you see that purple tree?" You cannot help but imagine a purple tree to make meaning out of the conversation! This book is designed to change your strategies of communication from blaming, to inspiring. Instead of "You never pay attention!" how about "What would it take for you to pay more attention?" The first statement is an accusation, and causes the listener to imagine a picture of not paying attention. The second example will cause the listener to imagine a picture of finding a way to pay more attention. This book will enable you, as a parent, to be more conscious of your communication and to be more focused on the outcome that you want.

Circumstances are always changing; it is important to learn to adapt. With these tools you will learn how to achieve your desired outcomes as well as add enjoyment to new challenges. The results will benefit you and everyone around you.

Let this book be an inspiration and a guide to you. You may find a wealth of beneficial information throughout the book. You will have access to effective communication tools to help you get through resistance, and to create more harmony and cooperation in your family. This will create a vehicle to tap into more of your children's powerful potential for growth.
Good Luck — Enjoy It!

Anna Russo
Your Life Coach

Dedication

I dedicate this book to all the people with whom I have worked; every one has been an inspiration to me to be more committed to this work. To my daughters, Rosanna and Lisa, who have been instruments of great learning and support. To my family for loving me unconditionally, always believing in me, and unafraid to give me the straight story. They have been patient through the years while I went through many classes and trainings. My gratitude goes to the many teachers in my life who have had a great impact on my personal and professional transformation. I want to thank my colleagues, particularly Laura Cuttica-Talice, for a mutual open exchange of ideas and strategies. Many thanks to Mary Roberts,M.A., who helped me set up the stage and was instrumental in the creation of the book! She has been eagerly waiting and consistently telling me that this publication was much needed in the schools as well as on an individual family level. I would like to express my gratitude to Lila Kadaj, M.F.A., for her encouragement and excitement. I highly appreciate my friend, Dr. Fred Vogel, for his effort, support and knowledge. Mostly I appreciate the many people whom I have coached, who have enabled me to witness their marvelous changes and accomplishments. Finally, to Rob for giving me the time and the space to accomplish this task and for appreciating my knowledge and independence.

Set Up the Stage/Overview

Through many years of working with people as a coach, particularly with children and teenagers who have difficulties concentrating or being motivated, I have made discoveries that have proven helpful for many of my clients. Growing up, I wish my parents had the skills that I'm revealing in this book! This is not about blaming parents, but about learning new strategies. Many resources were not available years ago; information is now readily accessible. You can learn and apply these strategies to create a happy, more harmonious family.

I grew up very shy and feeling unworthy. I promised myself that I would do things differently when I had my own family. Instead, I found myself repeating the same mistakes and creating and perpetuating the same family dynamics: anger, demands and yelling. I could not reach my children with the way I was communicating. I questioned my own reality, and realized there had to be a better way. Surely life had more to offer! I am sure you, as a reader, can relate to that. I went on a search, and through many classes, trainings, and the use of a personal coach, I began my transformation. I discovered that the message I received growing up had a major impact on my beliefs and actions. The more I searched, the more the quality of my communication began to change, as well as my self-worth, and the belief that there was hope.

You, as a parent, may sometimes wish there was a recipe for how to be a good parent. Since children are not born with an owner's manual, it takes research to figure out what works. You can probably relate to feelings of self-doubt and negative self-talk. "I didn't have good parents as a model." I don't have my own life in order – how can I help my kids? I'm at the end of my rope; I've done everything I know how to do, and it isn't helping. I don't know what else to do." Most people repeat the behavior they have learned because it is familiar. They operate under the belief that dealing with children is difficult, and they cannot win. Many people have negative self-talk about parenting.

That's what this book is about! I'd like to convey to you that it isn't about who is going to win; it is about producing results that are good for you and your family. The knowledge that I have gained has allowed me to assist people to develop themselves to live out their dreams.

Action Steps:

1. Be aware that you have all the resources inside you to make the changes you need to make. They need to be developed and brought out by a coach.
2. Make the decision to be the best you can be.
3. Commit to be better; don't just wish for improvement.
4. Focus on what you want to accomplish (instead of blaming); be result oriented.
5. Adjust your communication!

Every parent wants motivated kids! They want their kids to do well in school, clean their rooms, help out with chores, be self-motivated and take the initiative. Unfortunately, most of the time teenagers are not self-motivated; they are busy searching for their own identity.

Once, there was a belief that motivated people were born that way. Now we are discovering that motivated people can be created. People are driven to do what they find valuable and worthwhile. "What is the benefit of doing this?" is the underlying question that goes through the mind whether we are aware of it or not. This applies to all people.

As Maslow explained in his hierarchy of needs, we first take care of basic needs for food and shelter. Once those are in place, we look for love and connection. The next level is to define ourselves and find a place in the world. This occurs at any age, and it re-occurs throughout life as we go through this journey.

I invite you to consider for a moment the world of a young person. Young people have their own opinions of their lifetime experience, as we all do. They are in the process of discovering themselves, learning and defining who they are, sorting likes and dislikes, deciding what is important or not, and how to fit into their environment. Obviously, this process promotes concentrating on self, with very little concern for what the parents want or desire for them. They are working within their own frame of reference; it is their lifetime of experience. The frame of reference is different for everyone, and needs to be respected.

The parents often look at a child's apparent lack of motivation and communication and take it personally. They may feel guilty, assuming that they failed in some way. Some parents resort to threats to get short-term results, often passing on a negative legacy from their own childhood. Most people already know this doesn't change or help the situation. *At this point as a parent, you know how many different obstacles can get in the way of really reaching your teenager; you also know how important it is to do so. The following strategies will help to overcome these obstacles.*

CHAPTER 1

How to Remain Calm: The Importance of Taking a Deep Breath

Let's explore some of the factors involved in understanding how the transition from expectation to reality happens.

All of us, as couples, start out with a dream. We love each other and want to create our lives with a nice place to live, a perfect family and perfect children. We have an idea of what our lives should look like. Most of the time, our vision ends up leading to disappointment, pain, and a feeling of hopelessness, unless there is a plan for how to proceed.

Frame of Reference

Parents need to understand that children are copycats. They are born with no beliefs and no preconceived ideas. Children are born with strong curiosities, inquisitive minds and pay attention to their environment. They copy what they see and hear; generating feelings and opinions. They establish their own beliefs and make their own decisions, based on how they interpret their personal experiences (frame of reference). Children are great imitators; they model parents, relatives, friends and neighbors, television programs, and video games. This is how they learn their behavior. They learn to walk like their parents, talk like their parents, and behave like their friends or parents. This is how children develop social skills. This imitation by children is also referred to as "modeling". Children will model anybody and anything with which they come into contact. As they interpret various situations, they decide to be like whomever they are modeling, or decide to be just the opposite, even though they may not necessarily be aware of it. They do not consciously know that they can take pieces of various models and blend them to create their own model, which would work for their benefit and the benefit of everyone else involved in their life.

The Dream

Parents can hold tightly to the dream of the perfect family and ultimately will become inflexible. When they see a disobedient son or daughter, or a lack of interest and motivation, they feel frustrated and helpless. Parents may wish there were a magic wand to make everything better. Unfortunately, magic wands are not on the market!

The Approach

Changing this dynamic requires new skills, new strategies in communication, new behaviors and a new approach. When thinking about talking to a child, decide what you want the child to hear. **What result do you want?** Is your intention to have the child go away feeling bad just because you wanted to get something off your chest, or would you prefer asking non-judgmental questions to allow the child to open his or her mind and actually learn something from the situation? A good approach would be to ask:

"What are you hoping to accomplish?"
"What did you really mean by that?"

Wait for the response, because these questions make people think.

For example, what teenager has not threatened to kill herself and caused her parents to go into a panic? Some people say, "After all I do for you…" which causes guilt, creating more emotional pain. I know this is not the result the parents are looking for; they truly want to help, they just do not know how. There is an understandable knee-jerk reaction from the parents to what they perceive as a serious threat. However, in situations like this, we, as parents, can learn to focus. We can learn strategies to help us slow down. Instead of reacting to a child's drama, we can ask powerful questions like:

"What do you really need?"
"What is really going on with you?"
"What are you focusing on?"
"Can you focus on something that is going well in your life?"
"What would be a perfect day for you and the family?"

Once you ask the right questions, you will be able to understand what your children are trying to communicate to you, and you can help them get in touch with what they really want or mean. These are proven techniques that, in my experience, will help them to gain clarity on what they need, and what they really mean to say.

The Issue is Seldom the Issue

Here is an example of how asking the right questions can have a profound impact: I was coaching a 14-year-old who was not doing well in school and appeared to be depressed. When I asked her what was really going on with her, she answered that no one liked her. That's a pretty big statement, right? So, to my question, "Are you sure that no one likes you?" she replied, "I'm too shy and I don't have any friends." This is a completely different message than "no one likes me". I proceeded to ask her if she knew what she would have to do to make some friends. She responded that she did not know. I asked her if she had confidence in herself, would she be able to make friends? Her reply was, "That's it! If I felt good enough, I would be talking to more people." She was able to find confidence in some areas of her life, and used that confidence as a starting point for other areas.

I asked her to come back with three names and phone numbers. When she returned the following week, not only did she have the three names and numbers, but she had also gone to the movies over the weekend with one of the people on her list! Obviously, after that experience, she discovered more strength in herself; that she could work through her feelings of being shy. She was also more communicative and more open with her family. In other words, she was feeling good about herself, and it began to show up in many areas of her life. She got to know herself much better, and never mentioned that life was not worth living again.

Learn to Make Choices

Some of a child's behavior and responses come from modeling what he or she hears at home. If parents complain and bicker about little things, the children will pick up on the tone. They will formulate ideas and beliefs that it is hard to get cooperation, and the child ends up in emotional isolation. One couple would not kiss in front of their child. I asked them if their child saw only disagreement, would that be a balanced relationship? They saw the light: that it was okay to have disagreements, disappointments, and differences of opinions. They learned to live in a way that reflected respect and love for each other and all those around them. It is your choice, isn't it? You learned in a similar way; why pass on that legacy? Children are not really conscious of this process, and they end up confused, frustrated, and relying on drama to get their point across.

I invite you to think about the things you focus on in your life. This is not a war; take responsibility for the things you pick on, such as yelling and carrying on for a half hour over spilled milk. In the big scheme of things, will you remember the event five years from now? As the parent, **imagine taking a deep breath before you communicate**. How much calmer would you be? How much clearer would your message be? Would it change the way you invite the listener to pay attention, so that you can come to an agreement for a better outcome? How many problems and daily irritants would be eliminated or minimized if you took on this new approach?

CHAPTER TWO

How to Envision the Desired Outcome

I am aware that parents have the good intention to show love to their children. Most of us, as parents, want to express love and support to our children and encourage self-confidence, self-esteem, motivation, and pride in themselves and their accomplishments. Unfortunately, at times we have communication that is counterproductive.

Pitfalls

Some pitfalls of communication can occur directly or indirectly. Communication is not only talking. Communication is the ability to convey your ideas in a way that has the same meaning to you as it does to the listener. This principle applies to everyone in the situation.

Parents who were raised in a strict environment may try to compensate for their own childhood by giving too much freedom and very few guidelines to their children. In this situation, children often do not learn boundaries or respect for themselves or others. As a result, they may expect to have anything and everything they want at their command.

Are Children All The Same?

Different personality types respond differently to different communication styles. Here is an example: Imagine two children, each unique. One is very quiet and independent. The other is talkative and active, requiring more time and energy spent by the parents. The parents feel that dealing with the differences in each child's personality is too much work because the two personalities require different styles of communication. The parents complain, "Why can't you be like your brother/sister?" They are trying to make the two children carbon copies of each other. What happens to the child's self-esteem under these circumstances? Do you wonder if one would feel less loved?

I am suggesting now that the communication style needs to be different for the quiet, more introverted child. The parents in this situation can find something to compliment the child about so that the child feels good about herself. The parent can also invite the child to participate more with the rest of the family, and encourage more interactive activities. In her quiet way, this child may have something to offer to the higher-energy, more extroverted sibling. By initiating more group socializing, the parents will help the introverted child to explore new behaviors. The child who is always talkative and active can be invited to slow down and plan, to think about their communication, and finish their task.

Rules vs. Asking the Right Question

Parents have rules: "Do your homework," "Pick up your room," "Put your shoes away, and then you can go play." Children are very creative, so they find other things to do. Mom realizes that the chores were not done, so she takes away privileges (for example, television). Unhappy with the consequences, the children call to their dad, and he says it's okay to watch the television. This sends a message to the children that they can manipulate their parents, and do not have to be responsible for their own behavior. I invite you to think about what this does to the parents' relationship, as well as the patterns of manipulation that are being promoted in the child. In this case, the father needs to ask the child, "What caused you to lose the privilege of watching television?" This sends the child a clear message about responsibility, accountability and consequences.

As an adult, how do you respond when rules are imposed on you? Harmony and productivity can be achieved by making your children aware that everyone needs to participate; they not only have the ability, but also have the **responsibility** to listen and follow through. This is how you teach **boundaries** effectively.

No adult with common sense expects to get paid without working. Shouldn't we teach that concept to our children early? Just imagine how it would influence the quality of their thinking. I do not expect miracles; however, learning is inevitable with repetition. Imagine how much easier it would be for you to get your message across! You, as the parent, may have been frustrated in the past because you made a request to your child, got an answer, had to repeat the request again, and yet the task was still not done. The results did not match your expectations. In your mind, you have had enough. The time has come to raise your voice because you are angry, and you start exerting your authority. Have you found that you achieve better results when you start screaming? A famous saying is, "If what you are doing is not working, change what you are doing." Random actions do not guarantee success or desired results.

What Results Do You Want?

I wonder how your actions would change if your focus was on getting results and believing in your ability to get those results? How would you communicate? I invite you to keep focused on the outcome you want. As you do, your patience will increase so you can remain calmer and stay present to the situation.

I am convinced, if you are like me, that you have had experiences in your life where you have become frustrated because you were not sure about what to do or how to do it. When you let go of the frustration, you finally relax and your attitude changes. You may have then said to yourself, "Oh well, we'll see if this works." It was in that moment that your tension eased and you were able to access your own strength and gain the clarity needed to solve your dilemma.

Do you know how to do this?
What would it take for you to see yourself calmer, more focused, and present to the situation?

- **Would you focus on the problem or the result?**
- **Would you focus on the quality of your communication?**
- **Would you visualize coming to a mutual agreement**?

After you have done that, I can suggest more strategies for more effective communication. The first rule is to avoid closed-ended questions like, **"Do you have homework?"** This will only result in a yes or a no. What will the outcome be from there? Chances are it will lead to an argument.

My suggestion is for you to use open-ended questions such as, **"How much homework do you have?"** Pause, and wait for a response. Then ask, **"When are you going to start?"** Always wait for an answer; this is when patience is essential. Open-ended questions can be used in many circumstances. For instance, **"I noticed that your room has been neglected."** Pause. **"When were you planning on cleaning it?"** If there is no answer after you pause, you can initiate an agreement by saying, **"I expect to see it done by tomorrow night. Is that fair?"** You may even ask if they need assistance in organizing, or ask them what it would take to make their room feel like their very own. (Value their opinion.) Questions like this invite others to consciously or unconsciously recognize the respect they are getting. If you show someone respect, chances are that you are promoting good feelings. When people, both children and adults, feel good, they treat others better.

Essential Steps

- Envision the outcome that you want
- State it positively
- What would that outcome look like?
- Take a deep breath
- What steps need to be taken?
- Soften the tone of your voice
- Ask open-ended questions such as, "When would you like to do your chores?"
- Get an agreement
- Time frame
- Make a written list. It is useful for children and adults.

CHAPTER THREE

How to Eliminate Peer Pressure

Young people start to look outside of themselves and check out what other kids are doing. It becomes apparent around the age of ten to twelve, gets stronger as they get older, and continues through adulthood. If you look closely, you will notice this happening in other families. If it makes you feel better, you are not alone! Fashion is one of the many areas in which peer pressure shows up; children want the same clothes and games as their peers, whether the means to obtain them are there or not. Helping the children realize that what works in one family does not necessarily work in another, is one skill for which the parents can be responsible. The income, number of children, or the situation in general is most likely different for each family. Some parents feel bad about it, and some get defensive. Getting defensive only creates more determination on the young person's part to argue his or her point.

Beginning of Addictive Behavior

When we rely on things to make us happy, our happiness eventually requires more and more things to sustain that happiness. Society says that the difference between men and boys is the price of the toys. What are the children learning? Parents need to find their own strength and courage to address these issues by saying, **"I can appreciate**

that you want what your friends have. At this time it is not feasible for us. I'll see what I can do to get that particular pair of shoes for a special occasion or if you achieve a certain grade point." This way, the young person realizes she has to work toward a goal, and she has an active role in the process.

Drugs and Alcohol

Children look for approval from their peers. Some end up going to extremes; taking drugs or cutting themselves because it is what their friends are doing. Sometimes there are other reasons involved for these behaviors, which would have to be explored individually. In the case of seeking approval or a sense of belonging, children can fall innocently into groups where they feel accepted. In order to be part of the group, they start to exhibit the same behaviors. For example, a sixteen-year-old, who was a great softball player, moved in from another state. He enrolled in school and obviously joined the softball team. The players were sneaking beer and offered him a beer. He had never had beer before, as it was against his beliefs, besides being against the law at his age. He thought that to be on the team, he had to drink; otherwise they would not accept him. This behavior was disturbing him emotionally. His parents noticed a difference in his behavior and were very concerned and wanted to help him. He did not have the courage to tell his parents, so they were unaware of the true problem. When they brought him to see me, he told me what was bothering him. I asked him, **"What makes you drink when you are with them?"** His response was, "If I don't drink, they won't let me hang out with the group." He mentioned that he was the best player on the team, so I pointed out to him that, **"You are the best player and you don't drink."** After seeing the situation from this perspective he realized the importance of being appreciated for who you are and what you stand for. This new perspective gave him the strength he needed the next day after the game to turn down a beer. He said, "I play a good softball game. I don't drink." Children have a strong need to fit in, often overshadowing what they know is right. You may ask: Do you think you may lose one **true** friend by not doing…?

Some young people play sports and/or play an instrument because it is what a friend is doing. They are afraid if they do not participate, they will be looked down upon or they will miss out on something. The long time commitment of practice is not taken into consideration. They see athletes who win games and get recognition, but they are unaware of the long hours of practice and commitment that is put into achieving that level. Seeing only the end results, they wish for a miracle so they achieve the same results without putting in the effort. Producing good results requires applying ourselves; in other words, we must put forth the time and effort. Without the commitment, those results are wishful thinking. Parents need to understand their ability to present the whole picture to their son or daughter in a non-threatening manner, such as: **"Are you aware of the commitment?" "Are you willing to do the practice and be able to keep acceptable grades at the same time?"** (You decide what is acceptable.) The same questions apply to all other disciplines, from playing an instrument to having a lead role in a play, and everything in between.

Sometimes it is the case that just the opposite is true. For instance, children may not get involved in things they might enjoy and would be beneficial to them because they are afraid of not being able to measure up to their friends, or of being humiliated as they are gaining the skills necessary to be successful.

Be Flexible

Another scenario is that whatever the child has tried, he did not succeed, so he gave up. The parents of a fifth-grader named Luke contacted me before he began middle school band, because they were aware of his perfectionist tendencies, and did not want him to quit before he got started. They understood that if Luke had to embarrass himself in front of his peers, even though this learning process applied to all the kids, he would never continue in music. I suggested they think outside the box, and over the summer provide private lessons for him so that when he began school, he would have achieved a level of competence on the trombone. They followed my advice. Luke did well in music and three years later he is the first chair trombone player, is in the jazz band (audition only), and has won several scholarships to fine arts camps in Michigan. By the parents taking action and being in tune with Luke's needs, they were able to provide him with what he needed. (They gave him a head start!)

The private lessons Luke received that summer gave him the opportunity to overcome his fear of making mistakes in a new adventure. As a result, he was able to set up a strategy to succeed. He was not intimidated at playing in front of the class because he was more comfortable with his performance.

Another key factor involved in this situation is that a child in this scenario does not know how much time and effort his or her peers have put into practice, or the emotional discomfort the others went through. Encourage your child to ask her peers how they accomplished their goal. What did they do when they felt frustrated? Allow her to discover that talents need to be developed; they don't just happen.

CHAPTER FOUR

How to Motivate and Inspire Children and Teens

This scenario may sound familiar to you: You go to work, come home and find that the two things you had asked your son/daughter to do while you were at work, are not done. You may become verbally abusive, since your expectations were not met. In your mind, you feel that you are being taken advantage of because you are doing the best you can and your children are not being team players by taking on the responsibility to follow through. Eventually, you feel you have run out of things to say, bribing does not work, and you have reached the end of your rope. The verbal abuse is the last resort. By now, you are probably aware that becoming verbally abusive does not work. Some parents believe children have to respect adults no matter how abusive their behavior becomes. Is this your family legacy? Is this the behavior you would like your children to learn? Wouldn't it be better to say, **"I feel that this is getting out of balance,"** rather than blaming? Ask, **"How do you think we can work this out in a way that is fair to everyone?"**

As I mentioned earlier in another chapter, people are motivated by what they value. This applies to everyone. When faced with cleaning their bedroom or playing a game on the computer, which do you think most children would choose? I suspect the game on the computer will win hands down, unless you help them understand the value of having a clean room. A strong and primal value for people is pleasure. It is a natural tendency to move away from pain towards pleasure. If your child perceives cleaning the room as a painful experience, he or she will move towards the pleasure of playing a game. In this case, you can make sure that not cleaning the room could have consequences that are more painful than cleaning the room. To the child, it becomes time to look at what else is of high value to him. It could be having friends over in the evening. So, if you say firmly, **"Okay, since your room is not clean, you can't have friends over for a week or two."** Now you are using leverage with something that is important to him. Chances are, he will think about what he is going to do in the future, because having his friends over is just as important as playing a game on the computer. After the room is clean, tell him how good it looks. Do not say **"You missed a spot…"** because that negates everything he did. Ask him how good he feels about it. Use the three A's: appreciation, acceptance, and approval.

It Is the Way You Say It

I cannot count how many people have responded, "I tried that, and I've done everything." I can assure them that something is missing, because if they actually utilized the right techniques, they would have worked. Over the years, I have witnessed that these strategies have proven to be very successful for people who have applied them. People do not like to be wrong or are simply not aware that their method of communication is not effective. Sometimes an improvement in communication just takes a change in one word, a shift in the tone of voice, or switching from lecturing to asking questions. The voice reflects the attitude. If someone said to you that you were doing a poor job at work, it would sound like a lecture and a judgment. Would that cause you to get defensive? You would probably be more receptive to an observation like, "I noticed your performance has been lacking, and I know you can do better. What would you need to do to make sure your performance meets the expectations?" Have you noticed that when questions are used instead of statements, your mind is engaged and you become empowered to make a choice? If it works for you, it will also work for young people. Is the praise appropriate for what they do, or is it all blame?

If you take your child's negative behavior personally, you feel hurt because it may feel like she is undermining you. This thought pattern is not a good strategy. Remember that everyone is doing the best he or she can at any given time. Have you ever had a choice between work and fun? What would you do first? My point is, even adults push what they perceive as difficult or annoying chores and responsibilities to the last minute, and instead choose to do something more pleasant. If your attitude is directed toward envisioning the desired outcome of a situation, then you can look at the unfinished chore and think of approaching the situation differently. You could say, **"I noticed that your room is not clean. What got in the way?"** Anticipate that the child will come up with an excuse, but stay focused on the outcome and what you want to convey. This perspective will assist you in keeping your attitude light so you can continue and say, **"How soon will it be before you do** that?" and **"How long it will take for you to do that?"** If the answer is one hour, remind the child that an hour is very short period of time. Propose the question, **"Wouldn't it be worth doing it now and getting it out of the way so that you can be free for the rest of the evening?"** This way the child can move toward the pleasure of choosing what he or she wants to do after getting the work out of the way.

CASE STUDY:

Tony, a twelve-year-old boy, enjoys rollerblading with his friends. Every day he would come home from school, drop his backpack in the most inappropriate place, have his snack, and before his mother turned around he would already be out on the street meeting his friends to rollerblade for the next two and a half hours. He obviously has a very strong motivation for pleasure, and his grades were suffering as a result. Tony's mother would get upset every day about him not doing his homework. When he would come back to the house after rollerblading, he was tired and hungry again, and would spend only a half hour on his homework with very lousy concentration. Tony's obvious attitude was that doing homework put him out and was boring. Report cards are a strong measure of results; they do not lie about performance. Tony's report card reflected his lack of interest in his homework and his very poor performance.

Tony's mother, concerned about his attitude toward school and his lack of motivation, decided to get coaching for him. Although initially resistant, through my questions, he made some important discoveries about himself. I asked him, **"Do you know that your mother would like you to**

do your homework before you go rollerblading?" He answered that he knew that, but he preferred to go outside and do the activity with his friends. I asked him, "Do you enjoy it?" He replied yes, but he battled with himself for a long time. So I asked him, "While you are out there doing the activities that you enjoy, are you thinking about the fun you are having or something else?" He paused for a while and then replied, "I'm thinking about what my mom is going to say when I get home and how angry she is going to be." I asked him, "How do you know that?" He responded, "Because it happens every day."

I proceeded to ask more questions so he would gain insight about himself. **"Do you realize that although you choose to go out and play first, you are not free emotionally?"** Your mind is occupied thinking about the homework that is not getting done and your mother's arguments. Are you aware of how your body feels after playing so hard?" He looked very surprised, as if he had just realized something he had never thought about before. *While he was playing physically, his mind was on homework and consequences.*

I suggested to him to imagine himself getting home, having his snack, taking a few minutes to settle down, spending an hour and a half on his homework, and then going out to rollerblade with his friends. How much more would he enjoy playing without having homework and his mother's concern on his mind? As he imagined himself doing that he smiled and replied, "I would feel free for the rest of the night to enjoy what else I'm doing and be proud that I took care of what I had to do." His whole life changed. He started to notice that teachers were not yelling at him the next day, and they were actually friendlier toward him and complimented him on the change in his behavior. The discovery he made had changed his behavior and how he related to himself and the whole family. He realized that his choices impacted his whole life and every aspect of his environment.

Tony's mother was committed to supporting him, and as she observed the changes in his behavior, she was certain that she needed to keep him on track. She did this by reinforcing how proud she was of him because of his changes. She also kept asking him how he felt about the changes in his behavior, the improvement in his grades, and how much more peaceful it was around the house. The observations and questions that his mother had were very helpful for Tony to keep the good feelings alive, to continue to motivate him, and keep him going with his new behavior. Every time he thought about having his cake and eating it too, he would smile. He could play and do well in school. It was a matter of organizing his strategy.

I am wondering if by now you have realized that people are best motivated by utilizing their own motivational strategy. For Tony, his motivational strategy was to have free time and be able to play without the worries of the consequences of not doing his homework. Without those worries, he enjoyed his free time on a much deeper level, and got more satisfaction from it. For someone else, the motivational strategy might be gaining approval from adults. For some, the approval is the reward; for others it is the personal satisfaction of having accomplished something. Many people are motivated by money. If this is the case in your home, I recommend that money should not be the <u>only</u> reward. There are rewards that are much greater; you can link money with the satisfaction of doing a good job and the feeling of accomplishment.

Responses to Different Patterns of Behavior

A while back I suggested to one of my clients, who is a parent of a complex young man, that she ask her son what motivated him to do things. He bluntly told her what his motivation was. He said, "I don't like to see mess around me, and it makes me feel comfortable when the room is clean." He moved away from a mess and moved towards order and comfort. His strategy was self-satisfaction. My client's friend thought the same thing motivated her son, but she inquired anyway. When she asked, her son replied, "I know when I do my chores you don't complain, and I have the rest of the weekend to do what I want." So the first young man is more focused on self, and the second is more focused on others. According to your child's answer, you can direct your communication strategy to deal with the specific motivational factor. Referring to the first one, "Imagine how good **you** will feel after you do your chores". To the second one, "Imagine how **you** and the **people** around you will be impressed after you do… ?"

The old saying *walk your talk* shows up everywhere. Some parents spend way too much time preaching instead of inspiring their son or daughter. I know parents who forget that their children are people too, and they subject them to demands, yelling and screaming. Demands are not the way to get cooperation or positive responses. Children, like all people (whether they know it or not), like to get attention.

What is the quality of the attention they are getting? Any attention has an outcome, and they will learn to get more of what they are familiar with.

Here is an example: A mother who had a long day at work came home and immediately started cooking dinner and doing laundry, which required running back and forth from the kitchen to the laundry room. Naturally, she was feeling rushed and probably irritated. Isn't it time to change?

The Blaming Game

Mike, the fifteen-year-old son, happened to walk through the kitchen from the den (where he was doing homework) to get a glass of water. His mother, who was tired, started yelling, "Why aren't you helping? Can't you see how much I have to do?" She forgot that one hour ago she had told him that he had better do his homework before dinner. Mike was confused about the double message. He really did not notice how busy she was, because he was focused on his homework. It was also understandable for the mother to be frustrated and tired, and feeling that she could use some help. The best way to get help is to ask with kindness; it might go something like this. *"Mike, I know I requested that you get your homework done before dinner. Now I am realizing that I need help. I've got too much going on. So that we can have dinner at a reasonable time, would you set the table and mash the potatoes?"* This would be a request instead of a demand.

When you ask for help from your child, what is the first response you get? Rolling of the eyes, walking away, or grunting? If this is the case, I really encourage you to change your approach. With positive responses you know you have cooperation. When you use aggressive behavior, you know that whomever you are asking for help will be more resistant and less cooperative. So you may say under your breath, "Here we go again," and then yell, "I shouldn't have to ask you; you should know I need your help!" Before you know it, there is a full-blown argument, complete with blame and finger- pointing. The original objective to get some help is lost in the noise of the accusations. I wonder, in this scenario, what happened to the value that family is important. If you continue to do the same things the same way, you are guaranteed to get the same results.

Let us start with the basics. Most parents expect children to listen, follow through, and be good (whatever that means). Because they are doing a lot for their children, parents expect something in return. Ask yourself: When do I want my child to listen? **When is it important to follow through? What does 'being good' mean to me?** I hope you do not ask yourself these questions while you are driving. These are powerful questions that will engage your attention and allow you to gain clarity on what it is you really mean.

Stop for a moment and look at your own behavior. How many parents do you know who do not follow through, who ignore their partner's requests for help or cooperation, show resistance, show a lack of respect for the partner's opinion, or even worse, become argumentative because of their own need to be right? Is this familiar to you; do you intimately know anyone who fits into this category? Children are smarter than they are given credit for. Whose footsteps are they following in? In today's modern world with so much technology available and the speed of life going faster than we would have ever imagined ten years ago, we have had to adapt quickly to many changes. It is time we take a look at some of the changes we need to make as parents if we want to raise healthy and successful individuals.

The hardest thing to do is analyze our own behavior. We all like to think we are doing our best, and that we are doing the right thing. I do not doubt that you might be doing your best as you know it; however, I invite you to ask yourself, **"Is my strategy giving me the satisfaction and the results I want, or is there something better?" "Am I communicating with kindness and being a good role model?" "Is my behavior what I would want my kids to have?"** I am not implying that your behavior is wrong; I am simply inviting you to take a closer look at it. If your children were to mimic your behavior, what would your response be? Is there anything you would like to change in your behavior? Since behavior is all learned, it can be unlearned and changed to something more appropriate.

It is easier to identify resistance in other people; it is easy to spot when people are difficult to deal with. The hardest thing is to look at your own behavior. Starting now, there is an opportunity for you to examine your behavior and look at what you would like to change and what you want to keep. Imagine that you change your old behaviors of reacting to your children; showing you care, and making sure you convey that message to your son or daughter to whom you are speaking. Chances are you would talk to your children like you would the kids next door. You would pay attention to how you talk to them, what you say and your tone of voice. Have you ever wondered why you speak to the children next door kinder? Could it be that you want people to think that you are nice?

The Victim is Not Victorious

You may say, "It's easy for you to say, but when I'm frustrated, I lose it." Frustration is a result of expecting something to be different than it is. What you see is what is; your choice is to accept it or not. If it is not acceptable, I guarantee that your old approach will get you the same results. As I mentioned before, a new approach would be to take a deep breath so you can remain calm and see the situation from a new perspective. Then you could communicate with calmness and an open mind. Ask more questions instead of assuming and accusing. Listen with curiosity to the other person's point of view, and let her finish her sentence. Demonstrate by your behavior that you care, instead of being annoyed. When you are curious, your response will be more inspiring, even if you and your child do not agree: *"Mary, I can appreciate where you are coming from. Can you appreciate my suggestion and be open to try it out?"* You can see and feel that this question does not have pressure behind it, so people will be more inspired to work with you.

Studies have proven that the highest form of communication is behavior, and in most cases behavior becomes automatic. As you pay more attention, you become more conscious as to how you operate in the world, and then you have the freedom of choice to change some of your behaviors. Paying attention to your behavior is like buying a new car.

You never notice it on the road before you buy it, but after you purchase it, you see it everywhere!

CHAPTER FIVE

How to Promote Healthy Self-Esteem

Confidence and self-esteem are some of the most challenging areas in life we all must face. Self-esteem is the ability to believe in your self. Young people have many doubts about themselves; they aren't sure about who they are, their appearance, where and how they fit in, etc. All these doubts cause teens to internalize and personalize most of the experiences that they have. They need reassurance. You may think, *what are you talking about? I am always complimenting my kids.* However, your children may have a different perspective. How often have we heard the expression, what I said is not what you heard? Is it a complaint or balance? What is the intent of the complaint?

Family life will change when we give our children what they need. We tell them we love them, yet we also let them know what we do not like about their behavior. I recommend that you do not do this in the same breath. "I love you but you make me upset." This is something you can test for yourself. Try it in your own mind: *It's a beautiful day, but it's going to rain tonight.* Do you notice what happens to the beautiful day the moment you say *but*? The positive idea you previously had about the day is suddenly erased.

When people are unhappy with their children's behavior, they say, "I am upset with **you**." This negative comment about the person, rather than the behavior, could result in lowering the child's self-esteem. There is a difference between not liking the behavior versus not liking the person. The child starts to attach his identity to what he does; that means that he is only good enough if he does the "right" thing. The more appropriate expression would be, **"I don't like what you did,"** or, **"I don't like that you promise something and you don't follow through."** If your child comes home later than you requested and did not bother to call, the appropriate statement is, **"This is unacceptable behavior; what are you going to do about that in the future?"** Now you are referring to the action or lack of action instead of **attacking** the person. What they do and who they are is not one and the same. As people, whether children, teenagers, or adults, we are human, and that means we are valuable just as we are.

Behavior is learned; nobody is born knowing how to walk and talk or born with the capability to do any other task that we do as adults. Since we can all learn, we are all born with the ability to advance, and are good enough to excel. In most cases, people need guidance to discover their full potential. For example: Children may learn to procrastinate because they do not get the attention they want when they need it. If this is the case, the adults in their lives are modeling those behaviors **"Hold on; I'll be there in a minute!"** and the minute never comes.

When parents perceive that what their children promised does not match what they actually did, the parents may think of their children as being manipulative. This misperception likely leads to accusations and name-calling. The kids will withdraw to try to avoid conflict, or do the same thing over and over again to get the attention they are familiar with. I've seen this happen! In the long run this will create more pain, because the parents do not like those results either. The more demands placed on the children, the more they learn to be people-pleasers. Sometimes they will agree to a request only because they want to tell you what you want to hear. They are not thinking past that moment, and are certainly not thinking far enough in the future. Some children get plenty of attention, but they do not know when it is enough; they need to learn boundaries. We will refer to this in greater detail in the next chapter.

When parents notice that their child is shy or seems to be lacking interest, the parents might try to build self-esteem by reminding the child of how smart or how attractive he or she is. Have you ever done that? There is a good chance you ended up with the response of a glare from the child; did that surprise you? If your child does not feel good enough, she will not see herself as smart even though you know she is smart. She may not feel attractive and valuable. When you bring those issues up, she compares what you say to her feelings, and since she does not feel that way, she makes your statement wrong and translates it to your patronizing her.

One would get desired results by directing the communication in a way that opens the mind to the desired result. Let's explore this possibility. When people complain about low self-worth and low self-esteem, I usually ask questions like:

"Do you realize how much you have going for yourself?"

"Do you realize how smart you are?"

Questions like that make the brain go on a search whether people realize what you said or not. At this point they don't question anymore whether they are smart or not, they question if they **realize** that they are smart. The same applies to, **"Do you realize how beautiful you are?"** When they hear that, after they go inside on a search they may still say "no" but you will not get a glare at that point. You have a chance to ask the next question: **"What will it take for you to realize and accept that you are smart and attractive – you have a lot going for yourself!"** Over time, with caring and loving ways, you will be contributing to your children's development in a way that will lead to belief and trust in themselves, building higher self-esteem.

A Case Study in Low Self-Esteem

Mary (a young lady in the seventh grade) was having a lot of anxiety about her studies, although she was doing very well in school and getting straight A's. She studied four to five hours a day, every day. Her parents were concerned about the stress Mary was putting on herself. When she had to write a report, she would revise and change it at least five or six times. In Mary's mind, no amount of study was adequate to sufficiently prepare her for a test. Nothing seemed to be good enough. As time went on, this pattern got even stronger. The situation got to the point where her parents felt they needed to step in and do something to protect Mary's emotional well-being.

Through coaching, Mary discovered she did not believe in herself, and that her low self-esteem caused her to constantly worry and give herself negative suggestions, like, "I'm going to do poorly on the test, I don't know enough, "My report isn't good enough, "I have too much to do, I can't keep up", and "I can't remember this, because I'm not smart enough". In a nutshell, Mary's strategy was to focus on the negative, and it showed up in how she saw and talked to herself.

Mary also discovered that she constantly compared herself with other people, and never felt that she measured up to them. No matter what the reality, she felt she was less than they were. It was a vicious cycle.

I asked Mary **what was working in her life**. She replied that her parents loved, supported, and listened to her. She acknowledged that she was good in sports. When she started listing the positive things, she was actually surprised that she could find something positive to say about her life. With a smile, she said, "Thinking about these things feels good!" She recognized that she could actually feel better by focusing on the people and things she appreciated. The challenge would be to keep this up, and to integrate it into her daily patterns.

I asked her, what did she really want to manifest in her life? She said, **"I want to be happy, feel lighter, and get good grades."** My reply was that if she focuses on the negative and talks to herself in a negative way, she is going in the opposite direction of what she wants. It was an epiphany for her, and she expressed to me that she had never thought about it in that way.

I went on to explain that we get some reward out of every behavior. Rewards do not have to be positive; they are just results of our actions. When we think of a reward, we think of something positive, but every behavior produces results. To the question, **"What do you get out of all of this anxiety and pressure?"** Mary said, "It helps me to succeed, get good grades, and gain acceptance and attention."

I asked, **"Is there any other way that you could get those results without putting yourself through mental and emotional trauma?"** Her answer was, "I just realized by your question that if I stop focusing on what I can't do, and center more on what I know I can do, **I feel lighter."** She felt that if she concentrated on what she had instead of what she did not have, she would feel validated and loved. She acknowledged the importance of focusing on the positive. I asked her what the benefit would be for her if she changed those behaviors. Her reply was that she would lose anxiety, feel better about herself, and be more relaxed. I then asked Mary,

"How can you change your behavior and still succeed at getting the attention and acceptance that you need?"

She responded, "I have to believe in myself, remind myself that I'm smart enough, and that I feel proud of myself and my accomplishments. That would give me the courage to look at the real results. So far, all of the things I've been worrying about have worked out! As I keep focusing on positive things, I feel safe. That would change the quality of my life; I'd be less worried and I would feel lighter. My friends and family would see me stronger, outgoing, and happy. It would improve the quality of our relationships, as we would feel more comfortable together. That would lead to more respect from my loved ones, and more confidence in me."

CHAPTER SIX

How to Set Boundaries

Have you ever been exposed to families where everyone was talking at the same time or going in all different directions? I once knew a family with four children, and the parents did not seem to know how to establish boundaries. The children loudly made demands all at the same time, and the parents would jump from one plea to another. Boundaries and order were never established. No one in the family seemed to understand perimeters, nor did they have respect for other people's time or possessions. When they wanted something, the children screamed until they got it. As they got older, while getting ready for school, the children would put on their sibling's clothing without asking permission. Of course, if their sibling wanted to wear the same piece of clothing that day, you can imagine the scene that took place. Nobody bothered to step back and say, "If she wants to wear this today, it is her outfit! I had better decide to wear something else." The children had feelings of entitlement, and expected to be given what they wanted regardless of cost. If this did not happen, you could hear them from the next zip code.

The children's behavior had a major effect on their parents' relationship. They lived in a state of frustration, always walking on eggshells, always nervous about which child was going to have a tantrum next. There was no peace in the house. This family had a difficult lesson to learn. Although the parents' intention was to give their children unconditional love, in reality their indulgence of their children's behavior and constant providing of instant gratification created a chaotic environment where positive life lessons were not being taught, completely unrealistic expectations for the future were being instilled, and the children were being turned into selfish, narcissistic, frustrated human beings. Their environment at home had negative affects on their academic endeavors as well as their social abilities.

Promises, Promises

Another example is the story of Betty, a single mother. Betty would come home from work exhausted, her intention to care for two little ones. Even though she too had the best of intentions, when her children asked her for attention, she would put them off to get things done. Her response was usually, "We'll do that later." Later never came, so her daughters grew up with the belief that people did not have time for them. As they became teenagers, the girls tried to get attention in inappropriate ways. In school they dressed very suggestively, they spoke louder than necessary, they wore heavy makeup, and their circle of friends always fluctuated. Their attention span was very short and they did very poorly in school. Now the mother was facing major issues with both of them.

One day while driving to work after a frustrating meeting at school, Betty had a flashback of when her girls were young and would try to get her attention. She remembered making promises to them and not following through. With a little guilt she recognized that maybe all the inappropriate behavior and academic failures were results of her daughters' frustrations and disappointments. Betty now realized she had a lot of work ahead of her to change her daughters' strong need for attention.

Betty had a hard time concentrating at work that day trying to figure out how she could change the environment she had created at home. She was still at a loss. She realized she needed an outside influence (like a coach) to help her and her daughters and she decided to pursue that. She was very surprised by the first question of the coach to her daughter.

"How much attention do you get by doing badly in school?"

Betty realized, by her daughters' answers, that they received negative attention from the teachers and staff at school. They got attention from her because she had to take the morning off, to have the meeting at school that day. The next question was:

"Do you know any other way you can get attention?"

The girls were so acclimated to the same style of getting attention that they could not come up with an answer on their own. The coach made a suggestion to develop a strategy at home to stop and take the time to listen to each other and value the other's requests. She also suggested scheduling time to study for a certain period of time every day. A suggestion was also made to look around and notice the people who appreciated and valued them, such as grandparents and other family members. Betty and her daughters made a commitment to stick with the program. Within a short period of time, the family was communicating in significantly different ways.

Betty began hearing: "Thank you for doing this for me." "I wonder if you could help me out with my homework?" "Do you have time to help me out with dinner?" Once respectful communication was established, the reactive behavior was gone and the children's need for attention was achieved in a positive way.

Different Perspective

Peter and Ann have two teenagers and a second-grader: Ashley, Liz and Johnny. In the morning things get very chaotic. As the parents try to get ready to go to work, the children cannot find what they want to wear, and everyone blames each other. In the evening, things do not go much better. What drama! Johnny is a second-grader and needs help with his math. Liz is sixteen and wants the freedom to drive her friends around. Ashley is fourteen and needs a ride to soccer practice after school.

Mom and dad work long days and have demanding jobs. She knew she would be home later than usual that Monday. Mom asked Liz if she could do her a favor and drive her sister to soccer practice. Liz wanted to be free to drive around with her friends, and she was very resistant to her mother's request to help with the driving. Liz was testing her boundaries. It took some negotiation and a reminder that driving and using the family car was a privilege. Her mom reminded Liz of the importance of being a team player to break down her objections. Liz finally agreed and cooperated.

These have all been examples of how necessary and beneficial it is for children to have boundaries.

CHAPTER SEVEN

How to Give Your Child the Chance to Reflect/Think

Life is designed to push your bottom line. Your son or daughter is no exception. You know in your own mind that when someone does something unacceptable and you let it slide, the next time he or she will do it more emphatically. This will continue until you get frustrated and angry and then react. The situation does not have to get to that point. You can establish a foundation for good communication, mutual respect and accountability.

We usually listen to people we respect. Young people need to feel safe; they are actually looking for guidance and boundaries so they can feel safe within their perimeters. When you give children guidelines, they feel safe because they feel you care. At the same time, they may argue about something they want or want to do because they are trying to find themselves. You, as a parent, see that awkward behavior and may feel confused because it does not make a lot of sense.

The Power of the Right Question

Let us take Debbie as an example. She is a seventeen-year-old who drives her Mother's car to go shopping. On the way home one day, while she was driving twelve miles over the speed limit, the police stopped her and she got a citation. After giving the policeman her driver's license and registration, it was discovered that her mother had not signed the registration. When she walked in the house Debbie blamed her mother for getting the ticket, because she had not signed the registration. Her mother defended herself by accusing her daughter of not paying attention to her own driving. From the other room, the father heard the two shouting at each other, and realized that they were not getting anywhere. Before the argument escalated as it typically would, he called Debbie into the other room and started asking her questions:

Father: **"How did the policeman know from his car that the registration wasn't signed?"**
Debbie: **"Because he stopped me."**
Father: **"The reason was?"**
Debbie: **"I was going over the speed limit."**
Father: **"So do you realize how you participated in getting the ticket? I know not having the registration signed didn't help."**

Debbie looked at her dad without answering, but her expression spoke louder than any words she could say. Her dad proceeded to ask her, "What can you learn from this?" Again, silence and a look. Debbie's parents observed, however, in the following days, that she was quieter, observant, and attentive to what she was doing. Their communication improved, and they felt a lot safer bringing things up because they all recognized that communication is not about blaming. Communication is about learning from our experiences and finding solutions.

How Can We Do Things Better and More Effectively?

There is the million-dollar question! Can you remember something from six months ago that you reacted to because it seemed traumatic and you could not see your way out? You thought you were the only one in the world having that problem. Now, in retrospect, you are surprised you reacted that way. As a matter of fact, you do not even want to be reminded of your reaction. What has changed is your perspective. You are not caught up in the moment anymore, so you are able to be more objective. When you are objective, your emotions do not get tangled up in the situation. You are actually able to maintain your focus, take a deep breath, step back and remain calm - now your brain is free to see from a different perspective. Your strength is available to you and you can direct your attention toward a solution instead of the problem. The reality is that the situation is what it is; it has already occurred. The lesson you can learn from it is a valuable gift. When you learn something, you have it for the rest of your life. I guarantee you will never make the same mistake again. Tailgating is a prime example! The time comes when the car in front of you has to make a sudden stop. You will most likely leave more space between your car and the car in front of you in the future. If you do not learn from your mistakes, you will continue to behave in the same manner until the repeated negative consequences cause you to take notice and change.

Reacting by trying to make your son or daughter feel guilty will not change his or her behavior. That strategy is like a figure eight; it loops around and around with no learning taking place. Parents who let go of lecturing and preaching get better results. They replace those cyclical behaviors with questions which allow their children to think instead of getting defensive:

"What did you learn from this problem?"
"What results are you seeking?"
"To get those results, what do you have to do differently next time?"
"If this was happening to your best friend, what advice would you give him/her?"

These questions provide your children with an opportunity to see the bigger picture about what they are doing and where each step will take them. Joe came home an hour later than he promised he would, and he had a lot of homework. He stayed up until 11 p.m. to finish his homework. The next day, he was tired at school, and had a hard time focusing. That afternoon, he wanted to go out again after school. When his mom posed those questions he was upset at first, but quickly saw that he could make wiser decisions. Joe could see his friends, come home at a reasonable time and still get his homework done. He practiced that behavior for quite some time until it became second nature. His parents could count on him to be responsible for how he used his time and the decisions he made, and Joe felt he could count on seeing his friends three times a week.

CHAPTER EIGHT

How to Communicate with Different Personalities/Different Levels of Maturity

I am almost sure you are aware of this scenario: There are two children in a family who have their own personalities and different styles of communication. It is your belief that if you teach them the same things, and you provide them the same experiences, then they will both be clear about what you want. And yet, when you say something, one of them understands and follows the rules, and the other couldn't care less. You may be asking yourself in this situation, "Why aren't they getting it?" This is all too familiar, right?

The reality is that people have different personalities. Some are more open to exploration, and some start a behavior in which they keep doing the same thing although it does not prove beneficial. All individuals require a different approach. A young person who focuses on herself requires a different line of communication than someone who puts others above herself. Obviously, the best approach in life is to take into consideration both self and others.

Focus On Self

Mike, a twelve-year-old boy, has spent a lot of time watching television and playing computer games, and has not learned many social skills or good communication. His primary agenda was to cut communication with people short, so he could get back to his games. He actually had learned to focus on himself, do what he wanted when he wanted, and he argued back if he did not get his own way. He usually responded to his parents when they made a request:

- **"I'm** busy. I don't have time."
- **"I** don't want to do homework."
- **"I'm** not motivated."

Focus On Others

Mike's parents communicated with him the same way they did with his brother John (14 at the time) who had been much more involved with the family since he was a little boy. John used to ask his mom, **"Mom, can I help you with dinner?"** Not only did he make his bed and help his mom with dinner, he really enjoyed being involved in family life. His communication reflected that he was focusing on more than himself, like:

- "Dad, are **you** pleased with my grades?"
- "Dad, would it be okay with you if **we** do a project together?"
- "Can **we** watch TV together?"

Clearly, Mike sees what he wants and makes sure he protects his own interests above all else. John, on the other hand, includes his family with his interests. If you have experienced any of these scenarios (and I'm sure that some of you have) and tried everything you can think of to reach both children equally, now try this!

To move Mike in the right direction, the best approach is to tailor your communication to appeal to his style. When you want him to do something, address it in a way that gives him a benefit. More effective communication would be:

- "Mike, when will **you** have time? How can **you** make time?"
- "Mike, how proud would **you** be after you do your homework?"
- "Mike, what would have to happen for **you** to be motivated?"

You can communicate with Mike this way for a period of time, until he feels safe and understood. Eventually you can start adding **how everybody else would be pleased with changes in his behavior and proud of him.** Little by little, Mike will see how his new behavior will benefit him and everybody around him. He will understand that by acting respectful to himself and the environment, he does not have to lose a piece of himself. Mike would actually stretch his horizons, and be more fulfilled and happier.

In response to John, who is already focusing on other people by pleasing them all the time, the best approach would be:

- "I am very proud of you; are you pleased with your good grades?"
- "John, I want to do the project with you, but I will be late tonight. **Can you get it started, and I'll help you tomorrow?"** (Make sure you follow through the next day).
- "John, I enjoy your company, I appreciate who you are. I would be happy to watch some TV with you tonight!"

Addressing John this way would help John realize it is not enough to please other people, he also has to please himself and be proud of who he is and realize he can do things on his own. Both children are unique and special. They have different personalities, so they look at life differently. Mike has been looking at life through the lens of *how much can I get away with*, which has caused him to focus only on himself and become self-centered. Now he has an opportunity to look at how his behavior affects him and other people. He is also becoming more aware of his surroundings, which makes it easier for him to follow through. John used to please other people so much that he was afraid to do anything unless he got other people's approval. Now he has more strength because he is learning how important it is to approve of himself. The doubts he used to have about himself are diminishing. He feels more confident and more relaxed. He knows that as he continues to change, life will be more rewarding and meaningful.

Be Respectful of the Uniqueness

Children grow up at different stages; however, most parents believe their children should all act the same: well behaved and responsible. When this does not happen, they complain with an angry undertone. Boys are rough, girls are polite. How is this teaching acceptance and individuality?

Mr. and Mrs. Smith have three children, a girl and two boys. Natalie had been meticulous about herself, her chores, her work and her belongings since she was a little girl. Her two brothers, Matt (the youngest) and Mark (the oldest) behaved quite differently. Mark seemed to have a hard time being responsible. Matt and Mark showed more interest in sports and running with their friends. They were not interested in keeping things neat and organized.

Mrs. Smith had been making two mistakes. One is that she was not telling Natalie, "I am proud of you because of how well organized and responsible you are." The other mistake is that she would tell the boys, "Why can't you be like your sister? Look at her; she gets excellent grades. I never have to tell her to clean her room. She is respectful and polite around adults."

This approach caused Natalie to feel that she was responsible for her brothers development. At the same time, her brothers were building resentment toward Natalie, blaming her for their mother's dissatisfaction. As time went on, Natalie started to complain about the lack of acknowledgment. Her mother's response to the complaint was, "You should know that I appreciate you and what you do!" Sometimes this happens in families; they hear about things only when something is going wrong. The things that are working usually do not get acknowledged. The lack of feedback from her mother caused Natalie a lot of unnecessary stress.

Having gotten sick and tired of the complaints from their mother, the boys decided to take a different approach. They started to do things that irritated Natalie, causing the kids to compete against each other. Matt and Mark were becoming aware that their friends were getting good grades and taking responsibility for their chores. They noticed that their friends were rewarded with things they wanted, and had more privileges. This awareness motivated the boys to be like their friends. As a result, the dynamics between them and their mother changed.

The mother felt a little guilty when she realized that the kids matured at different times. She wondered if she had been putting too much pressure on the boys by pushing them to be like their sister. The mother knows now that instead of asking them, "Why can't you be like your sister" she would have been more effective in getting cooperation rather than resistance from the boys if she had asked questions like:

"What's important to you?"
"Is it important to have good grades?"
"What are you willing to do to get what you want?"
"Do you see any value in getting your chores done?"

In a previous chapter, I mentioned that even if they answer, "I get money," you know what their values are and you can use the answer they give you to create the next question.

With all due respect, most parents think they are doing the right thing. You can gauge whether or not that is true by observing the results your strategies yield. When the results are far from your expectations, chances are the situation needs a different approach. It may be encouragement, or more questions in a direction that helps the other person think, and come up with his or her own conclusion. You can use force or threats, and they may get you results for a little while, but not long-term changes. When people realize that what they do is an expression of themselves, they put a lot more effort into what they do. A friend of mine used to say to his kids, "Can you get through the day?" Everyone gets through the day, one way or another. What is the quality of that day? Have you ever asked yourself that question?

Design the Results

Each day we lay the foundation for the next. After reading this book and using the techniques suggested, you may realize that hoping for things to change on their own without making any personal changes just does not happen. We can hope for the weather to change; we do not have control over that. "I hope my situation changes," is a recipe for disappointment. That thought implies that you have no control over your life. **"What will it take for my situation to change?", involves personal participation.** To reach people, good communication is necessary; that requires work. Is your family important enough to put the time and energy into it? If you bought a plant, there is a strong chance you would not water it with milk. Milk is a liquid, but not the one that helps plants grow. Everybody communicates; the quality of the communication determines the strength of the message. Good communication requires the communicator:

- To be clear with his or her message.
- To know the outcome that he or she is moving towards.
- To state the communication in the positive.
- To stay oriented toward the desired results.
- To keep in mind that the end result is good for everyone involved.

Remember to breathe before you speak, especially when things look as though they are not going the way you would like them to. You may have heard the words of wisdom: *count to ten.* This technique is similar; it gives people the chance to step back and not get caught up in the heat of the moment. Appreciate and accept your child's growth, and continue to adapt to the physical and emotional maturity he or she is achieving.

Avoid The Grandparent Syndrome
Some grandparents often think of their grandchildren as just kids. Although this may be amusing to adults, it can be irritating and frustrating to teenagers because of their strong need for acceptance and appreciation for what they have accomplished. Can the grandparents stretch and see their grandchildren going through the stages of development, and be supportive in a way that matches their

accomplishments? This can actually be instrumental in encouraging them.

CHAPTER NINE

How to Keep Rapport

Rapport is the ability to connect and relate to people. Body language, tone of voice, showing compassion, and carefully choosing your words are all things that greatly affect rapport. Studies have shown that as human beings, we use our five senses to communicate: sight, sound, touch, taste and smell. Our senses are called modalities, or modes of how we see, hear, and feel about the world. We use all our senses, but the majority of people establish one preferred mode. They keep using the favored sense repeatedly, without an awareness of doing so.

Example:

- "I see what you're saying" would be the sight mode.
- "I told you!" would be the sound mode.
- "My feelings are hurt" would be the touch mode.
- "It left a bad taste in my mouth," or "I need a vacation so badly I can taste it" would be the taste mode in conjunction with the touch mode, which is not mentioned directly.
- "The sweet smell of success" or "I smell a rat" would be the smell mode.

Bad feelings are an indication of looking at something in a negative way, in addition to negative self-talk, of which we are usually unaware. To change those bad feelings, we need to become conscious of what we see and what we say to ourselves. Some people do not ever ask themselves questions like, **"If I feel bad about this, what am I looking at that is causing these bad feelings? How am I looking at this? Do I even have a choice about my feelings?"** These questions are seldom available unless we learn we can change our feelings by changing the way we look at things and the way we talk to ourselves. To get out of a bad feeling we need to go into either a visual mode, or change the message we give ourselves. In general, people try to change a feeling by replacing it with another feeling. This strategy very seldom works. The easiest way to change a feeling is to take a look at the situation from a different perspective and to have different self-talk.

Open Your Awareness

Have you ever wondered while feeling bad, what it is you are focusing on? What is causing the discomfort? Is it possible that you do not want to give in to what you need to do; that you would rather do something else? Or worse yet, you interpreted somebody else's request as a demand; consequently, it caused you to react. It is important for all of us to pay attention to what is going on inside our mind. Reacting and getting angry about something usually means that we feel powerless, and that someone else is in control. We like to have choices. Now put yourself in someone else's shoes when he or she has been told to do something, and feels like doing something else. What usually happens? Every one of us can relate to that in one way or another.

If parents insist on using their authority, they may create more resistance. When parents gain rapport with their children, they usually get the desired results and more cooperation; they invite children to see things from a different perspective. I know many people who use constant lecturing to get through to their kids. They use the 'keep talking approach' and have no idea if what they are doing is working or what to do next.

A messy room, difficulty concentrating, and doing poorly in school: these are all indications of a lack of visual imagination and negative self-talk. Let us focus on one of these issues. If his or her room is messy, chances are your child feels bad already. When you yell, "Why haven't you cleaned your room?" more bad feelings and guilt are promoted, alienating him or her even further. This breaks rapport. What if, instead, you posed the question:

"Have you noticed how messy your room is?"
"What stops you from cleaning your room?"

Conversation would be initiated and your child would be engaging in it. You can then use the child's answer to formulate your next question. The more information you gather, the more clear you both become on what to avoid and what strategy to move toward. Hypothetically, if the answer is, "Cleaning my room is work, and after school I don't want to be working," you now know how the child feels about cleaning his or her room. With a little finesse and a caring tone of voice, you can ask:

"Do you like to see your room clean and organized?"

Most children would answer "no" to get out of the task (avoidance pattern). You proceed with the next question:

"Imagine if I said 'no' if you asked me to drive you someplace you wanted or needed to go? How would you feel?"

This question helps the child to see the situation from a different perspective, which allows him or her to lighten up. After that, you proceed with:

- "When your room is clean what are the benefits?"
- "Isn't it easier to get ready in the morning when you know where your things are and you can find them easily?"

Again, you can continue to create a bigger picture of how connected everything is: family, school, and friends. The benefits of having a system that works in life will become apparent.

Keep An Open Mind

Bad grades or a lack of interest are signs of not having the brain organized systematically. Brenda was a sixth-grader with low self-esteem. She did not feel good enough about herself and she had a lot of negative self-talk. She would sit in a classroom and tell herself she did not understand the material; she attached bad feelings to the class and to the teacher. She would go home and have a hard time doing homework, due to the general feelings she had about not being smart enough. Her mother had the best of intentions and tried to help her, but it was not working. She would say, "You should do better – you're a smart girl!" Frustrated, her mother sought help, and that is when she realized her communication was not helping her daughter.

I asked Brenda how she saw herself. She did not have a clue. "What do you say to yourself in general?" She was not aware of that either. So, I simplified:

- "Do you see yourself as being smart?" She raised her eyes up, a sign she was beginning to visualize.
- "What do you say to yourself?" Her answer was, "I'm not smart enough."
- I then asked her, "Can you change it to 'I am smart!' And her reply was, "That feels better!"
- "What resources do you have to maintain this vision of yourself, and continue to say, **'I'm smart enough to learn!"**
- When she heard "I'm smart enough to learn!" she let out a major sigh. She gained the insight that when something was presented to her, she had the belief that she should already know it. So I responded to her, **"Imagine if you were expected to walk before you ever started to walk – would you have ever walked?"** Logically it did not make sense, it made her laugh and helped her change the belief that she had to know something before she was even exposed to it.
- The next question I asked was, **"What resources do you still need to be able to see yourself as confident**

to learn and say, 'I am smart' on a consistent basis?" She replied that she needed some tutoring. It was hard for her to catch up.

Coaching enabled her to see herself differently and with more confidence, and the appropriate self-talk generated good feelings and a lightness about her, so she started to believe in herself. She was so excited that she decided to use this same strategy in every aspect of her life. In the classroom she was able to focus because she was not concerned about being good enough anymore; she knew she was. This made it easy for her to concentrate on the task at hand. Her attitude changed, she participated and asked questions in the classroom. She was more attentive to her chores after school. Her overall communication was smooth and engaging. Her mother was happy and surprised that she had found an answer to her frustration. Her daughter was doing so well that her mother expressed to me, "I never thought that she would turn things around. I thought I had to wait until she was eighteen."

These same questions can be applied to the messy room, and any other situation you want to change. By asking these questions, not only do you help your children balance their strategies for success, but you also assist them to become more autonomous. You help them create a map for them to follow. Treating resistance with threats very seldom creates the desired response, not to mention that whatever cooperation you do get will not last. That tactic teaches your children to move only if there is an immediate negative consequence. I am assuming that as a parent, you want lasting changes. Numerous people have benefited from these kinds of questions, have built rapport, and have gained a closer and more respectful relationship with their families.

You can build rapport easily when you watch people. If they get distracted, instead of yelling, ask them, "What were you supposed to be doing right now?" Watch how quickly they get back on track.

These strategies will assist you to engage in communication with your children to connect with and learn more about them, and they will feel more relaxed. Children want to know you rather than know about you. They want you to know them; they need to know you are interested in their hopes and dreams. When you give up lecturing and start to ask more questions, you build healthier relationships. Rapport shows them that you care. **You do realize the power of questions.** It is also beneficial for you to know where your kids are coming from, and figure out a way to close the gaps. When they make a mistake, maintain the rapport by reminding them of what they did well, instead of, "Here you go again! Nothing is working." It is much more respectful if one would say, "You made a mistake. You have made them before, and you turned it around. I'm sure that you can turn this around, can't you?" Just think about the effect that would have on you. It works the same way with your youngster and yourself.

CHAPTER TEN

How to Communicate in Combined Families

Do you know what the divorce rate is? It was 55% a couple of years ago; and although it has decreased slightly, the numbers are still staggering. It has become a fact of life that when a couple gets married, chances are each will be bringing children into the relationship from previous marriages. This message is even highlighted in some movies! These children have been raised in two different environments (more than likely), with different parenting systems. After the parents are divorced, each parent may meet someone else and begin a new relationship. The beginning of a relationship is also like the experience of a new infant; when the baby is born, everyone makes a fuss over it and life is wonderful. Later, the destructive patterns occur. The honeymoon phase of a new relationship is one in which you are both wonderful, and the dynamic of the relationship has not been established. There are indications of patterns that people do not like about their partners children but for the most part, the parents tend to overlook them as they bask in "wonderful." When they all come together, and the novelty has worn off, people start to look at the reality of the situation and begin to complain, "Can you believe what **your** kids did!"

Some people have not resolved the initial anger and frustration that was built up during a failed marriage and the custody battles. Sometimes the kids end up paying the price for the unresolved issues and emotional baggage that their parents carry. Every situation is teaching us something. If we learn the lesson, it helps us mature; if not, the blaming continues. It usually takes two people to make or break a relationship. If we know what to look for, the signs are usually there that tell whether a relationship will work or not. This book is not about resolving marital problems, although the strategies help in every area in life.

Lacking Objectivity

Jenny was divorced for a couple of years before she met her current husband, Mike. She had two girls, and in her eyes they were perfect. Mike brought a boy and a girl into the marriage. While they were dating, Jenny would chuckle at the antics of Mike's children. Deep down, however, she was judging their behavior; she couldn't believe some of the things they would do. Yet, she always made excuses for the behavior of her two girls. After they all came together, Mike shared joint custody with his ex-wife, and Jenny obtained full custody with paternal visitation every other weekend. Since they lived within a reasonable distance, Mike's children did not have to change schools, so they were with their dad three days a week, and every other weekend.

Once the families started spending some real time together, interesting dynamics began to occur. Jenny became increasingly frustrated at her new husband's children, and viewed their behavior - coming in the house with muddy shoes and forgetting what she considered to be the basic requirements of life – as appalling and disrespectful. Mike became frustrated with Jenny's treatment of his children, and resented the excuses and lack of objectivity she displayed when it came to her girls. Things began to heat up at home. Jenny came to me for coaching because the levels of anger and irritation at home were no longer tolerable. I asked her to step out of herself and view Mike's kids' behavior from a neutral perspective, then from the same place, view her daughters' behavior. Her response was that she realized she was treating the children very differently, because she felt protective of her girls; that was what her mother did, and that was what she was going to do. Jenny had a hard time letting go of her judgments and the need to be right. Although this is not an uncommon response from a parent in a blended family, it is a destructive behavioral pattern to fall into. I'm happy to say that Jenny does not represent the majority of blended families.

Here is the story of a couple that got married with six kids between them. Before they married, they realized some preparation was crucial for a smooth melding of the families. They came to me with this kind of preparation in mind, and we discussed what was important to them, their goals and their dreams for the future. We talked about their flexibility levels; what was acceptable and what was intolerable. I presented strategies to help them maintain objectivity with each other's children, such as looking at behaviors from a neutral position. I suggested weekly family meetings, where both the successful and unsuccessful results could be discussed, and where a list could be made detailing their strategy on how to go about improving whatever they agreed to work on that week. When they did come together, they were ready for the challenges ahead, and it went as smoothly as it could have possibly gone, even though this family was larger than the family in the previous paragraph.

There is a lot to be learned from these two examples. Jenny and Mike thought that if they were good people with good intentions, things would work out. In most cases, you have to put in time and energy, and use a formula that has been proven over and over to produce the results that you want. Clearly, the second family realized they needed to add some skills to their positive intentions. They valued their children and their relationship enough to invest in it and make it a priority.

Recipe to Follow to Ensure Success:

- Think before reacting.
- Step back and ask yourself, "What's the best thing to do in this situation?"
- What do I really like about this person? (If you focus on that, the rest goes away.)
- If this situation involved my best friend, what advice would I give? Follow that advice.
- Promise to treat friends, family, and your spouse with appreciation, acceptance and approval.

Give yourself permission to use these strategies with yourself as well, and lead by example.

I hope you derive from this book the same enjoyment I got out of writing it, and that the tools will provide you with the benefits you are looking for. This is a good start and only the beginning of what is possible! I look forward to hearing your feedback on how this book has improved your ability to communicate with your children; leading to peace, respect, and a happier family life. You can visit my website at: www.successstrategiesnlp.com or email me at: annaru@comcast.net.

ADDITIONAL EMPOWERMENT TOOLS AVAILABLE BY ANNA RUSSO

AUDIO

TURN FEAR INTO CONFIDENCE

BE YOUR IDEAL WEIGHT

LIFE CHANGES – ANNA RUSSO and FRED VOGAL
Change Past Stresses into Resourcefulness

STOP SMOKING

ULTIMATE REST AND RELAXATION

ACCESSING YOUR OWN POWER – ANNA RUSSO and KAREN MacDONALD

For assistance with your selection, contact us at www. successstrategiesnlp.com or email at annaru@comcast.net

About the Author

Anna Russo is one of the top certified trainers in the field of Neuro-Linguistic Programming (NLP). Born and raised in Italy, Anna attended the school Magistrale a Cassino Provincia di Frosinone. Russo has achieved international recognition for her development of many successful programs for individual behavioral change and enhancement. Her reputation is that of one who achieves rapid and powerful results with her own style of innovative and personalized change work. Her career includes 30+ years of experience in teaching, business ownership and life coach. Among her students are corporate presidents and vice-presidents, physicians, social workers, sales managers and representatives, as well as families and individuals seeking personal change. The creator of *Success Strategies*, Russo is also the author of Connecting With Resistant Teenagers, many articles, the producer of goal-setting CDs, and has made numerous TV and radio appearances. She has addressed and conducted training sessions for groups ranging from educational institutions to multi-million-dollar companies.

Her education includes a Degree in Education from Italy and three-and-a-half years of studies in psychology. Certifications consist of: NLP Master Trainer; graduate of Resource Training Institute; and Life Coach since 1990. Russo is the past president and a current member of IMDHA, a member of the Troy Chamber of Commerce, and Professional Women in Business. Some of the larger companies and institutions she has taught classes at are

AAA, John Hancock, UAW Ford, Macomb Community College, Adult Education Classes, Beaver Aerospace, and the Rehabilitation Strategies Center. She has also conducted retreats for hospitals and provided many in-service workshops for school systems.